SISTE

MW00639172

The Amazing Secret
Purgatory

children
of
Medjugorje

© 2011 by Children of Medjugorje, Inc.
All rights reserved.

Republished in 2020.
Book Design by Catholic Way Publishing.

Children of Medjugorje, Inc — Bosnia Herzegovina, 2011.

Translated from French by Anne Laboe.
Cover: Nancy Cleland, United States.

The American version is published by Queenship Publishing, USA. 1997
www.queenship.org

The original version is in French. www.editions-beatitudes.fr

Distribution: see website www.sremmanuel.org This book is also translated into:
Italian, Spanish, Dutch, Portuguese, Polish, Romanian, Slovakian, Indonesian,
Croatian and Arabic.

Ordering Information:
Orders by trade bookstores and wholesalers.
Please contact Ingram Content at www.ingramcontent.com

ISBN-13: 978-0-9980218-6-7

11 10 9 8 7 6 5 4 3 2

Available in E-Book.

www.childrenofmedjugorje.com

Contents

Introduction

Maria Simma is an Austrian mystic: by a particular gift from God, as has already been seen in the history of the Church, she has been receiving visits from souls in Purgatory. What do these souls say? They issue warnings; they ask for prayers and speak of the inexpressible sufferings of Purgatory, eased by the joyful expectation and certainty of finding themselves, sooner or later, in the arms of God. They reveal to us, the living, the immense power we have to relieve the sufferings of the deceased and to receive in exchange a great deal of assistance and a number of benefits, in this life and in the next.

The testimonies reported by Sister Emmanuel in this book, taken from Maria Simma's own lips, offer much food for thought. They will be able to help us change our attitudes and habits, and to start living in a different way, according to the desires of God.

The Lord uses many channels to speak to His children each day and to help them in their spiritual needs. The gifts that the Lord gives to privileged souls are like powerful lighthouses which illuminate the paths of men.

Let us make good use of this!

FATHER MATTEO LA GRUA OFM

Theologian

On the way to beatification

Foreword

This Booklet Fills a Void

One day, I read with great interest a book about the souls in Purgatory and it struck me a lot because it related very recent testimonies. Besides that, it explained very well the Church doctrine on the subject. It is a book by Maria Simma. Straight away, I wrote to the publisher, who told me that Maria Simma was still alive (since then she has returned to the Father - March 2004). Quickly I contacted her and she agreed to meet me in order to answer my questions of which I had many!

I was delighted because each time I had the opportunity to speak about the poor souls, I noticed that there is an immense interest on the part of my listeners. Often, they beg me to tell them more, pushing me further, asking me, "Tell us more Sister, tell us other things about these souls!" And I see clearly that this fulfills a vital thirst, it fills a void. It answers a critical question, a fundamental question: What is waiting for us after death?

It must be said too, that these things are rarely taught any more in parishes, in regular catechism, practically not taught

anywhere at all. So, there is a great emptiness, a great ignorance, even a certain anguish in the face of these realities.

Therefore, this sharing of mine will help us not only to get
rid of this anguish once and for all with regard to Purgatory;
it will also enlighten us, enable us to understand that God's
plan for us, for our destiny, is absolutely magnificent, splendid. We have in our hands an immense power on this earth
to give happiness to the souls of our departed and to find that
happiness for ourselves as well in our lives.

Who is Maria Simma?

She was a simple peasant woman of Sonntag, a very lovely
village in Austria. Because of the great poverty of her family,
her brothers had to work at a very young age to make a
living. The daughters were put in the service of rich families.
Since her childhood, Maria had prayed a great deal for the
souls in Purgatory. When she was twenty-five, she was unex-
pectedly favoured with a very special charism in the Church,
very rare actually, the charism of being visited by souls in
Purgatory. She was a fervent Catholic and she had a great
humility. This struck me a lot. In spite of the extraordinary
character of her charism, she was living alone and very poorly
in her father's house. I met her in this home in 1989, then
again in 1991. For example, in her little room we hardly had
enough space to move around the chairs she offered us . . .

An extraordinary charism? Yes, but which obviously has
deep roots in the history of the Church, for many are the

saints, canonized or not, who have experienced this charism. I could mention for example, St Gertrude, St Catherine of Genoa who wrote much on the subject, Maryam of Jesus and Margaret Mary Alacoque, Paray-le Monial (France) who had the vision of the Sacred Heart of Jesus, the Holy Cure of Ars, Saint Faustina of Poland, St John Bosco, Blessed Maryam of Bethlehem and so on. When we look closely at the teachings of these Saints, we see that all of them say the same thing. Maria Simma, for her part, only relives their beautiful testimonies.

This is why I did not hesitate to interview her as she was willing to make herself available. You can easily imagine that I swamped her with questions; I made the most of it.

For the sake of brevity and clarity, I had to summarize some of Maria's testimonies; at other times, I give you her own words. Here and there you will also find my own personal comments and quotations from various saints.

The Holy Bible tells us:

"All then blessed the ways of the Lord; the upright judge who brings hidden things to light, and gave themselves to prayer, begging that the sin committed might be completely forgiven. Next the valiant Judas urged the soldiers to keep themselves free from all sin, having seen with their own eyes the effects of the sin of those who had fallen.

After this he took a collection from them individually, amounting to nearly two thousand drachmas, and sent it to Jerusalem to have it offered as a sacrifice for sin. An action altogether fine and noble, prompted by his belief in the resurrection! For had he not expected the fallen to rise again, it would have been superfluous and foolish to pray for the dead, whereas if he had in view the splendid recompense reserved for those who make a pious end, the thought was holy and devout. Hence he had this expiatory sacrifice offered for the dead, so that they might be released from their sin." (2 Mac 12: 41-45)

The Church tells us:

"Our prayer for them is capable not only of helping them, but also of making their intercession for us effective." (Catechism of the Catholic Church, § 958)

The Liturgy of the Mass contains this prayer:

Remember also our brothers and Sisters,

Who have fallen asleep in the hope of the resurrection, And all who have died in your mercy;

Welcome them into the light of your face. Have mercy on us all, we pray,

That with the Blessed Virgin Mary, the Holy Mother of God,

With the blessed Apostles

And all the saints who have pleased you throughout the ages,

We may merit to be coheirs to eternal life,

And may praise and glorify you through your Son Jesus Christ.

Amen.

The Interview with Maria Simma

1. The First Time

Maria, can you tell us how you were visited for the first time by a soul in Purgatory?

Yes, in 1940. One night, around three or four o'clock in the morning, I heard someone coming into my bedroom. This woke me up, I looked to see who on earth could have walked into my bedroom.

Were you afraid?

No, I was not at all fearful.

So that night . . . tell us!

Well, I saw a complete stranger, he walked back and forth slowly, I said to him severely: "How did you get in here?

Go away." But he continued to walk impatiently around the bedroom as if he had not heard. So, I asked him again, "What are you doing?" But as he still didn't answer, I jumped out of bed and tried to grab him, but I grabbed only air! There was nothing there. So, I went back to bed but again I heard him pacing back and forth.

I wondered how I could see this man, but I couldn't grab him. I rose again to hold onto him and stop him walking around. Again, I grasped only emptiness.

Puzzled, I went back to bed. He didn't come back but I couldn't get back to sleep. The next day after Mass, I went to see my spiritual director and told him everything. He told me that if this should happen again, I should not ask "Who are you?" but "What do you want from me?"

The following night, the man returned, definitely the same man. I asked him, "What do you want from me?" He replied, "Have three Masses celebrated for me and I will be delivered."

So, I understood that it was a soul in Purgatory. My spiritual father confirmed this.

He also advised me never to turn away the poor souls but to accept with generosity, whatever they asked of me.

And afterwards, did the visits continue?

Yes, for years, there were only three or four souls, above all in November. Afterwards, there were more.

2. A Love Wound

And what do these souls ask of you?

In most cases, they ask to have masses celebrated and that one is present at these Masses. They ask to have the rosary said and also that one makes the Stations of the Cross.

At this point, the major question is raised: What exactly is Purgatory? I would say that it is a marvelous invention of God. Let me give you an image. Suppose that one day, a door opens and a splendid being appears, extremely beautiful, with a beauty that has never been seen on earth. You are fascinated; overwhelmed by this being of light and beauty, even more so that this being is madly in love with you. You have never dreamed of being loved so much and the fire of love which burns in your heart impels you to throw yourself into his arms.

But wait — you realize at this moment that you have not washed for months and months and that you smell! Your nose is running, your hair is greasy and matted, there are big dirty stains on your clothes so you say to yourself, "No, I just can't present myself in this state. First, I must go and wash, have a good shower, and then straight away I will come back."

But the love which has been born in your heart is so intense, so burning, so strong, that this delay for the shower is absolutely unbearable and the pain of the absence, even if it only lasts for a couple of minutes is an atrocious wound in the heart, proportional to the intensity of the revelation of the love — it is a "love wound."

Purgatory is exactly this. It's a delay imposed by our impurity, a delay before God's embrace. A wound of love which causes intense suffering, a waiting if you like, a nostalgia for love. It is precisely this burning, this longing which cleanses us of whatever is still impure in us. Purgatory is a place of desire, a mad desire for God, desire for this God whom we already know for we have seen him but with whom we are not yet united.

Now I am going to ask Maria to clarify a fundamental point:

Maria, do the souls in Purgatory nevertheless have joy and hope in the midst of their suffering?

Yes, no soul would want to come back from Purgatory to the earth. They have knowledge which is infinitely beyond ours. They really could not decide to return to the darkness of the earth.

Here we see the difference from the suffering that we know on earth. In Purgatory, even if the pain of the soul is terrible, there is a certitude of living forever with God. It is an unshakable certitude. The joy is greater than the pain. There is nothing on earth which could make them want to live here again, where one is never sure of anything.

Maria, can you tell us now, if it is God who sends a soul into Purgatory, or if the soul itself decides to go there?

It is the soul itself which wants to go to Purgatory in order to be pure before going to Heaven.

The souls in Purgatory adhere fully to God's will. They rejoice in the good, they desire our good and they love very much, they love God and they love us too. They are perfectly united to the spirit of God, the light of God.

Maria, at the moment of death does one see God in full light or in an obscure manner?

In a manner still obscure but all the same in such brightness that this is enough to cause great longing.

Actually, it is such a dazzling brightness compared with the darkness of the earth! And it is still nothing compared with the full light that the soul will know when it arrives in Heaven. Here we can refer to "near death experiences." The soul is so drawn by this light that it is agony for it to return to earth in its body after this experience.

3. Charity Covers a Multitude of Sins

Maria, can you tell us what the role of Our Lady is with the
souls in Purgatory?

She comes often to console them and to tell them they
have done many good things, she encourages them.

Are there any days in particular on which she delivers them?

Yes, above all Christmas day, All Saints day, Good Friday,
the Feast of the Assumption and the Ascension of Jesus.

Maria, why does one go to Purgatory, what are the sins
which most lead to Purgatory?

Sins against charity, against the love of one's neighbour,
hardness of heart, hostilities, slandering, calumny, all
these things.

Saying wicked things and calumny are among the worst
blemishes which require a long purification?

Yes!

Here Maria gives us a very striking example which I would
like to share with you.

She had been asked to find out if a woman and a man were in Purgatory.

To the great astonishment of those who had asked, the woman was already in Heaven and the man was in Purgatory. In fact, this woman had already died while undergoing an abortion whereas the man often went to Church and apparently led a worthy devout life.

So, Maria searched for more information, thinking she had been mistaken, but no, it was true. They had died at practically the same moment but the woman had experienced deep repentance and was very humble whereas the man criticized everyone. He was always complaining and saying bad things about others. This is why his Purgatory lasted so long and Maria concluded, "We must not judge on appearances."

Other sins against charity are all our rejections of certain people we do not like, our refusals to make peace, our refusals to forgive and all the bitterness we store inside.

Maria also illustrated this point with another example which gives us food for thought. It is the story of a woman she knew very well. This lady died and was in Purgatory but in the most terrible Purgatory with the most atrocious sufferings and when she came to see Maria, she explained why. She had a female friend, which between them arose a great enmity, caused by herself. She had maintained this enmity for years and years even though her friend had asked many times for peace, for reconciliation but each time she refused. When she fell gravely ill, she continued to close her heart, to refuse the reconciliation offered by her friend right up to her death bed. I believe that this example has great significance concerning bitter grudges which we harbor and our words too can be destructive, we can never emphasise enough how much a critical or bitter word can truly kill but also on the contrary how much a word can heal.

Maria, please tell us, who are those who have the greatest chance of going straight to Heaven?

Those who have a good heart towards everyone. Love covers a multitude of sins.

Yes, Saint Paul himself tells us this!

What are the means which we can take on earth to avoid Purgatory and go straight to Heaven?

We must do a great deal for the souls in Purgatory, for they help us in their turn. We must have much humility, this is the greatest weapon against evil, against the evil one, and humility drives evil away.

I cannot resist telling you a very lovely testimony of Father Berlioux (who wrote a wonderful book on the souls in Purgatory), concerning the help offered by these souls to those who relieve them by their prayer and sufferings.

He tells the story of a person, particularly devoted to the poor souls, who had consecrated her life to their relief.

"At the hour of her death, she was attacked with fury by the devil who saw her at the point of escaping from him. It seemed that the entire abyss was united against her, surrounding her with its infernal troupes.

The dying woman struggled incredibly for some time when suddenly she saw, entering her apartment, a crowd of unknown people of dazzling beauty, who put the devil to flight and approaching her bed, spoke to her with the most heavenly encouragement and consolations. With her last breath in great joy she cried, "Who are you? Who are you, please, you who do so much good to me?"

The benevolent visitors replied, "We are inhabitants of heaven, whom your help has led to Beatitude and we in our turn come in gratitude to help you cross the threshold of eternity and rescue you from this place of anguish, to bring you into the joy of the Holy City."

At these words, a smile lit up the face of the dying woman, her eyes closed and she fell asleep in the peace of the Lord. Her soul, pure as a dove, presented to the Lord of Lords, found as many protectors and advocates as souls she had delivered and recognized worthy of glory, she entered in triumph among the applause and blessing of all those she had rescued from Purgatory. May we, one day, have the same happiness!"

The souls delivered by our prayer are extremely grateful. They help us in our lives, it is most perceptible. I strongly recommend that you experience this yourself. They do help us; they know our needs and they obtain many graces for us.

Maria, I am thinking of the good thief, who was next to
Jesus on the cross. I really would like to know what he did
for Jesus to promise him that this very day, he would be in
the Kingdom with Him?

> He humbly accepted his suffering, saying that it was jus-
> tice and he encouraged the other thief to accept his too.
> He had the fear of God which means humility.

Another beautiful example of this is related by Maria Simma.
It shows how a good action makes up for a whole life of sin.
Let's hear it from Maria herself:

> "I knew a young man of about twenty in a nearby village;
> this young man's village had been cruelly stricken by a se-
> ries of avalanches which had killed a large number
> of people.
>
> One night this young man was at his parents when he
> heard an avalanche just next door to his house. He heard
> piercing screams, heartrending screams, save us, come
> save us, we are trapped beneath the avalanche.
>
> Leaping up he rose from his bed and rushed down-
> stairs to go to the rescue of these people. His mother had
> heard the screams and prevented him from leaving. She
> blocked the door saying, "No, let others go and help
> them, not always us. It's too dangerous outside; I don't
> want yet another death." But because he had been deeply
> affected by these screams, he really wanted to go to the
> rescue of these people. He pushed his mother aside, he
> said to her, "Yes, I am going, I can't let them die like this."

He went out and then he himself on the path was struck by an avalanche and was killed.

Three days after his death, he comes to visit me at night and he says to me, "Have three masses said for me, through this, I will be delivered from purgatory." I went to inform his family and friends. They were astonished to know that after only three masses, he would be delivered from Purgatory. His friends said to me, "Oh, I would not have liked to be in his place in the moment of death, if you had seen all the bad things he had done."

But this young man said to me, "You see, I have made an act of pure love in risking my life for these people. It is thanks to this that the Lord welcomed me so quickly into His heaven. Yes, charity covers a multitude of sins . . ."

The story of this young man shows us that charity, a single act of love given freely, had been sufficient to purify this young man from a dissolute life and the Lord had made the most of this moment of love. Maria added to that story that this young man may never again have had the opportunity to offer such a great act of love and that he may have turned bad. The Lord in His mercy took him just at the moment when he appeared before Him at his most beautiful, most pure, because of this act of love.

It is very important at the hour of death to abandon ourselves to God's will.

Maria told me of the case of a mother of four children who was about to die. Instead of rebelling and worrying she said to the Lord, "I accept death as long as it is Your will and I put my life in Your hands. I entrust my sons to You and I know that You will take care of them."

Maria said that because of her immense trust in God, this woman went straight to Heaven and avoided Purgatory.

Therefore, we really can say that love, humility and abandonment to God are the three golden keys to going directly to Heaven.

4. Offer a Mass for Them

Maria, can you tell us what are the most effective means to help deliver the souls from Purgatory?

The most efficient means is the Mass.

Why the Mass?

Because it is Christ who offers Himself out of love for us. It is the offering of Christ Himself to God, the most beautiful offering. The priest is God's representative but it is God Himself who offers Himself and sacrifices Himself for us. The efficacy of the Mass for the deceased is even greater for those who attached great value to the Mass during their lives. If they attended Mass and prayed with all their hearts, if they went to Mass on weekdays — according to their time available — they draw great profit from Masses celebrated for them. Here, one harvests what one has sown.

A soul in Purgatory sees very clearly on the day of his funeral if we really pray for him or if we have simply made an act of presence to show we are there. The poor souls also say that tears are no good to them, only prayer. Often, they complain that people go to a funeral without addressing a single prayer to God while shedding many tears, this is useless!

Concerning the Mass, here is a beautiful example given by the Holy Cure of Ars (France), to his parishioners. He told them this:

"My children, a good priest had the unhappiness to lose a friend he cherished greatly and so he prayed very much for the repose of his soul.

"One day God made known to him that his friend was in Purgatory and he suffered greatly. The holy priest believed that he could do no better than to offer the Holy Sacrifice of the Mass for his dear friend who had died. At the moment of the consecration, he took the host between his fingers and said, 'Holy Eternal Father, let us make an exchange. You hold the soul of my friend who is in Purgatory and I hold the Body of Your Son in my hands. Well, good and merciful Father, deliver my friend and I offer Your Son with all the merits of His death and passion.'

"The request was answered. In fact, at the moment of the elevation, he saw the soul of his friend shining in glory, rising to Heaven. God had accepted the deal.

"My children, when we want to deliver from Purgatory, a soul dear to us, let us do the same. Let us offer to God through the Holy Sacrifice, His beloved Son with all the merits of His passion and death. He will not be able to refuse us anything."

5. Don't Waste Your Earthly Sufferings

There is another means, very powerful, to help the poor souls: the offering of our sufferings, our penance such as fasting, renunciations, etc — and of course involuntary suffering like illness or mourning.

Maria, you have been invited many times to suffer for the poor souls, in order to deliver them. Can you tell us what you have experienced and undergone during these times?

The first time, the soul asked me if I wouldn't mind suffering for three hours in my body for her and that afterwards I could resume working. I said to myself: "If it will all be over after three hours; I will accept it." During these three hours, I had the impression that they lasted three days, it was so painful. But at the end, I looked at my watch and I saw that it had only lasted three hours. The soul told me that by accepting that suffering with love for three hours, I had saved her twenty years of Purgatory!

Yes, but why did you suffer for only three hours to avoid twenty years of Purgatory? What did your sufferings have that were worth more?

It is because suffering on earth does not have the same value. On earth, when we suffer, we can grow in love, we can gain merits, which is not the case with the suffering in Purgatory. In Purgatory the sufferings serve only to purify us from sin. On earth we have all the graces; we have the freedom to choose.

All this is so encouraging because it gives an extraordinary meaning to our sufferings; the suffering which is offered, voluntary or involuntary, even the smallest sacrifices we can make, suffering of sickness, mourning, disappointments, if we live them with patience, if we welcome them in humility, these sufferings can have an inconceivable power to help souls.

The best thing to do, Maria tells us, is to unite our sufferings to those of Jesus by placing them in the hands of Mary. She is the one who knows best how to use them since often, we ourselves do not know the most urgent needs around us.

All this of course, Mary will give back to us at the hour of our death.

You see this suffering offered will be our most precious treasures in the other world. We must remind each other of this and encourage each other when we suffer.

6. And Don't Begrudge Your Prayers

Another very effective means, Maria tells us, is the Stations of the Cross because by contemplating the sufferings of the Lord, we begin little by little to hate sin and to desire salvation for all people. And this inclination of the heart brings great relief to the souls in Purgatory.

The Stations of the Cross also move us to repentance; we start repenting when faced with sin.

Another thing very helpful to the souls in Purgatory is to pray the rosary, all fifteen mysteries, for the sake of the deceased. Through the rosary many souls are delivered from Purgatory each year. It must be said here as well that it is the Mother of God herself who comes to Purgatory to deliver the souls. This is very beautiful because the souls in Purgatory call Our Lady "the Mother of Mercy."

The souls also tell Maria that indulgences have a value that we cannot calculate for their deliverance. It is sometimes cruel of us not to make use of this treasure that the Church proposes for the profit of souls. The subject of indulgences would be too long to explain here, but I can refer you to the marvelous text written by Pope Paul VI in 1968 on this. (See page 76).

Therefore, we can say that the great means of helping the souls in Purgatory is prayer in general; all kinds of prayer. Here I would like to give you the testimony of Hermann Cohen, a Jewish artist who converted to Catholicism in 1864 and greatly venerated the Eucharist. He left the world to enter a very austere religious Order and he frequently adored the Blessed Sacrament for which he had a great veneration. During his adoration he would beg the Lord to convert his mother whom he loved so much. Well, his mother died without having been converted. So, Hermann, sick with sorrow, prostrated himself before the Blessed Sacrament and in deep grief prayed: "Lord, I owe you everything, it is true, but what have I refused you? My youth, my hopes in the world, my wellbeing, the joys of a family, a rest? I sacrificed all as soon as You called me; and You, Lord, Eternal Goodness, who promised to give back a hundredfold, you have refused me the soul of my mother. My God, I succumb to this martyrdom, I will stop my complaints." He cried his poor heart out. Suddenly, a mysterious voice struck his ear:

"Man of little faith, your mother is saved! Know that prayer is all-powerful in my presence. I gathered all those you have addressed to me for your mother and my providence took account of her in her last hour.

"At the moment she expired I came to her; she saw me and cried: 'My Lord and my God!' Have courage, your mother has avoided damnation, and fervent supplication will soon deliver her soul from the bonds of Purgatory."

We know that Father Hermann Cohen, soon afterwards, learned through a second apparition that his mother had risen to Heaven.

I also strongly recommend the prayers of Saint Bridget for the poor souls. You may find them at your Catholic bookstore.

Let me add something important: the souls in Purgatory can no longer do anything for themselves, they are totally helpless. If the living do not pray for them, they are totally abandoned. Therefore, it is very important to realize the immense power, the incredible power that each one of us has in his hands to relieve these souls who suffer.

We wouldn't think twice about helping a child who has fallen in front of us from a tree and who has broken his bones. Of course, we would do everything for him and immediately! So, in the same way we should take great care of these souls who expect everything from us, attentive to the slightest offering, hopeful for the least of our prayers, to relieve them from their pain. It might be the finest way to practice charity.

I think for example of the kindness of the Good Samaritan in the Gospel, towards the man left half dead on the roadside, bleeding from his wounds. This man depended completely on the good heart of the passerby.

Maria, why can one no longer gain merits in Purgatory when one can on earth?

Because at the moment of death, the time to earn merits is over, for as long as we are living on earth, we can repair the evil we have done. The souls in Purgatory envy us this opportunity. Even the angels are jealous of us for we have the possibility of growing for as long as we are on earth.

But often, the suffering in our lives leads us to rebellion and we have great difficulty in accepting and living it. How can we live suffering so that it bears fruit?

Sufferings are the greatest proof of the love of God, if we offer them well, they can win many souls.

But how can we welcome suffering as a gift and not as a punishment (as we often do), or even as a chastisement?

We must give everything to Our Lady. She is the one who knows best who needs such and such an offering in order to be saved.

On the subject of suffering I would like to relate a testimony that Maria told. It was in 1954, and a series of deadly avalanches had struck a village next to Maria's. Later other avalanches struck but they were stopped in a completely miraculous way before reaching the village so that there was no damage.

The souls explained that in this village, a woman had died who had been ill and was not properly treated. She had suffered terribly for thirty years and she had offered all her sufferings for the sake of her village.

The souls explained to Maria that it was thanks to the offering of this woman that the village had been spared from the avalanches.

She had borne her sufferings with patience. Maria told us that if she had enjoyed good health, the village could not have been saved. She adds that sufferings borne with patience can save more souls than prayer, (but prayer helps us bear our suffering).

We should not always consider suffering as a punishment; it can be accepted as atonement not only for ourselves but above all for others. Christ was innocence itself and He suffered the most for the atonement for our sins.

Only in Heaven will we know all that we have obtained by suffering with patience in union with the sufferings of Christ.

Maria, do the souls in Purgatory rebel when faced with their suffering?

No! They want to purify themselves; they understand that it is necessary.

7. At the Point of Death

What is the role of contrition or repentance at the moment of death?

Contrition is very important; the sins are forgiven but there remains the consequence of the sins. If one wishes to receive a full indulgence at the moment of death —that means going straight to Heaven — the soul has to be free from all attachment.

Here, I would like to share a very significant testimony given by Maria. She was asked to find out about a woman that her relatives believed to be lost, because she had led an awful life. Well she had had an accident, she fell from a train, and this accident killed her. A soul told Maria that this woman had been saved, saved from Hell, because at the moment of death, she said to God, "Lord, You are right to take my life because in this way, I will no longer be able to offend You." And this erased all her sins. This example is highly significant, for it shows that a single moment of humility, of repentance at the moment of death can save us. This does not mean that she did not go to Purgatory but she avoided Hell which she perhaps deserved through her impiety.

Maria, I would like to ask you: at the moment of death, is there a time in which the soul still has a chance to turn

towards God, even after a sinful life, before entering into
eternity — a time if you like between apparent death
(medical death) and real death?

Yes, yes, the Lord gives several minutes to each one in order to regret his sins and to decide: I accept or I do not
accept to go and see God. There we see a film of our lives.

I knew a man who believed in the Church teachings
but not in eternal life. One day he fell gravely ill and slid
into a coma. He saw himself in a room with a board on
which all his deeds were written, the good and the bad.
Then the board disappeared as well as the walls of the
room and it was infinitely beautiful. Then he woke up
from his coma and he decided to change his life.

Maria, at the moment of death, does God reveal himself with
the same intensity to all souls?

Each one is given knowledge of his life and also the
sufferings to come; but it's not the same for everyone. The
intensity of the Lord's revelation depends on each
one's life.

Maria, does the devil have permission to attack us at the
moment of death?

Yes, but man also has the grace to resist him, to push him
away, so if man does not want anything to do with him,
the devil can do nothing.

That's good news! When someone knows he is going to die soon, what is the best way for him to get prepared?

To abandon himself totally to the Lord. Offer all his sufferings. Be completely happy in God.

What attitude should we have towards someone who is going to die? What is the best that we can do for him?

Pray hard! Prepare him for death. One must speak the truth.

Maria, what advice would you give to anyone who wants to become a saint here on earth?

Be very humble. We must not be occupied with ourselves. Pride is evil's greatest trap.

Maria, please tell us: can we ask the Lord to do our Purgatory on earth in order not to have to do it after death?

Yes, I knew a priest and a young woman who were both ill with tuberculosis in the hospital. The young woman said to the priest: "Let's ask the Lord to be able to suffer on earth as much as necessary in order to go straight to Heaven."

The priest replied that he himself didn't dare to ask for this. Nearby was a religious Sister who had overheard the whole conversation. The young woman died first, the priest died later and he appeared to the Sister saying: "If only I had had the same trust as this young woman, I too would have gone straight to Heaven."

Thank you, Maria, for this lovely testimony.

At this point, Maria asked for a five minute break, as she had to go and feed her chickens... But the minute she returned we continue with our questions.

8. The "Inhabitants" of Purgatory

Maria, are there different degrees in Purgatory?

Yes, there is a great difference of degree of moral suffering. Each soul has a unique suffering particular to it; there are many degrees.

Do the poor souls know what is going to happen in the world?

Yes, not everything but many things.

Do these souls tell you sometimes what is going to happen?

> They simply say that there is something around the corner but they don't say what, they only say what is necessary for people's conversion.

Maria, are the sufferings in Purgatory more painful than the most painful sufferings on earth?

> Yes, but in a symbolic way. It hurts more in the soul.

I guess it's very difficult to describe . . . Does Jesus himself come to Purgatory?

> No soul has ever told me so; it is the Mother of God who comes. Once I asked a poor soul if she could go to look for a soul I had been asked to find out about. She replied, "It is the Mother of Mercy who tells us about it"
>
> Also, the souls in Heaven do not come to Purgatory. On the other hand, the angels are there: Saint Michael... And each soul has its guardian angel with it.

Fantastic! The angels are with us . . . But what do the angels do in Purgatory?

> They relieve suffering and provide comfort. The souls can even see them.

Amazing! If this goes on Maria, you're almost going to make me want to go to Purgatory with all these stories of angels! Another question: you know, many people today believe in reincarnation. What do the souls tell you concerning this subject?

The souls say that God gives only one life.

But some would say that just one life is not enough to know God and to have the time to be really converted, that it isn't fair. What would you reply to them?

All people have an interior faith, I mean in their conscience; even if they don't practice. They recognize God implicitly. Someone who does not believe — that does not exist! Each soul has a conscience to recognize good and evil, a conscience given by God, an inner knowledge — in different degrees of course, but each one knows how to discern good from evil. With this conscience, each soul can become blessed.

What happens to people who have committed suicide? Have you ever been visited by any of them?

Up to now, I have never encountered the case of a suicide who was lost — but this does not mean, of course that that doesn't exist but often the souls tell me that the most guilty were those around them, when they were negligent or spread calumny.

At this moment, I asked Maria if the souls regretted having committed suicide. She answered yes. Often, suicide is due to illness.

These souls do regret their act because as they see things in the light of God, they understand instantly all the graces that were in store for them during the time remaining for them to live — and they do see this time which remained for them, sometimes months or years — and they also see all the souls they could have helped by offering the rest of their lives to God. In the end, what hurts them most is to see the good that they could have done but did not because they shortened their lives. But when the cause is illness, the Lord takes this into account of course.

Maria, have you been visited by souls who have destroyed themselves by drugs, overdosing for example?

Yes, but they are not lost, it all depends on the cause of their drug taking, but they must suffer in Purgatory.

If I tell you for example that "I suffer too much in my body, in my heart, that it's too hard for me to take it and that I wish to die," what can I do?

This is very frequent. I would say, "My God, I can offer this suffering to save souls," this gives renewed faith and courage. But no one says this anymore nowadays. We can also say that in doing this the soul gains a great beatitude, a great happiness for Heaven. In Heaven there are thousands of different types of happiness, but each one is a complete happiness; all desires are fulfilled. Each one knows he deserves no more.

Maria, I would like to ask you: have people from other religions — for example, Jews — come to visit you?

Yes, they are happy. Anyone who lives his faith well is happy, but it is through the Catholic faith that we gain the most for Heaven.

Maria, are sects or cults bad for the soul?

Sects are very, very evil; everything must be done to bring people out of them.

Are there priests in Purgatory?

There are many. They did not promote respect for the Eucharist, so faith overall suffers. They are often in Purgatory for having neglected prayer, which has diminished their faith. But there are also many who have gone straight to Heaven.

What would you say then to a priest who really wants to live according to the heart of God?

I would advise him to pray much to the Holy Spirit and to say his rosary every day.

Maria, are there any children in Purgatory?

Yes, but Purgatory for them is not very long or painful since they lack much discernment.

I believe certain children have come to visit you; you were telling me the story of this little child, the youngest one you saw, a little girl of four. But tell me why was she in Purgatory?

Because she had received from her parents a doll as a Christmas present. She had a twin Sister who had also received a doll.

This little four-year-old girl had broken her doll. Then, secretly, knowing that no one was watching her, she went to put her broken doll in the place of her Sister's, swapping them, knowing full well in her little heart that she was going to upset her little Sister — and she knew very well too that it was a lie and an injustice. Because of this, the poor girl had to do Purgatory.

In fact, children often have a more tender conscience than adults. It is necessary above all with them to combat lying. They are very sensitive to truth or untruth.

Maria, how can parents help to form the conscience of their children?

> Firstly, through good example, this is the most important. Then through prayer. Parents must bless their children and instruct them well in the things of God.

Very important! Have you been visited by souls who on earth practiced perversions? I am thinking for example about the sexual domain.

> Yes, they are not lost but they have much to suffer to be purified. For example, homosexuality truly comes from the evil one.

What advice would you give then to all those people afflicted by homosexuality, suffering from this tendency?

> Pray a lot for the strength to turn away from it. They should above all pray to the Archangel Michael; he is the great fighter par excellence against the evil one.

And people love him! Maria, what are the attitudes of heart which can lead us to losing our soul for good, I mean going to hell?

> It is when the soul does not want to go towards God, when it actually says, "I do not want to."

THE AMAZING SECRET OF PURGATORY   39

Thank you, Maria, for making this very clear.

Here I would like to mention something. I questioned Vicka on this, one of the visionaries in Medjugorje, who also told me that those who go to hell, and she has seen hell herself, are only those who decide to go there. It is not God who puts someone in hell. On the contrary, He is the Saviour, He begs the soul to welcome His mercy and the sin against the Holy Spirit which Jesus speaks of and which cannot be forgiven is the absolute refusal of mercy and this in full awareness, full conscience. Pope John Paul II explained this very well in his letter on mercy. Here too we can do so much with prayer for souls in danger of being lost.

Maria, would you have a story illustrating this?

One day, I was on a train and in my compartment, there was a man who didn't stop speaking evil of the Church, of priests, even of God. I said to him, "Listen, you don't have the right to say all that, it is not good." He was furious with me. Afterwards, I arrived at my station, I got off the train and I said to God, "Lord, do not let this soul be lost."

Years later, the soul of this man came to visit me. He told me that he had come very close to hell but he was saved simply by this prayer I had said at that moment.

It is great to see that just one thought, one impulse of heart, a simple prayer for someone, can prevent them from falling into hell. It is pride which leads to hell. Hell is to say no to God with stubbornness. Our prayers can inspire an act of humility in the dying, a single instant of humility, however small, and this can help them to avoid hell.

But Maria, how can one actually say no to God at the moment of death when one sees Him?

For example, a man once told me that he did not want to go to Heaven. Why? "Because God accepts injustice," he said. I told him that it was man, not God. He said, "I hope that I do not meet God after my death or I will kill Him with an axe!"

He had a deep hatred of God. God grants man free will. He wishes each one to have his free choice.

God gives to everyone during his life on earth and at the hour of his death, sufficient grace for conversion, even after a life spent in darkness. If one asks for forgiveness sincerely, of course one can be saved.

Maria, Jesus said that it was difficult for a rich person to enter into the Kingdom of Heaven. Have you come across such cases?

Yes, but if they do good works, works of charity, if they practice love, they can get there, just like the poor.

Praise God! Maria, do you still have visits from souls in Purgatory?

Yes, two or three times a week.

Really! What do you think of the practices of spiritism, for example séances, calling on the spirits of the departed, Ouija boards etc?

It is not good. It is always evil; it is the devil who makes the table move.

It is so important to say this again and again. People really need to hear this, because nowadays more than ever, these evil practices are increasing dangerously.

Maria, please tell us what is the difference between what you are experiencing with the souls of the departed and those practices of spiritism?

We are not supposed to summon up the souls; I don't try to get them to come. In spiritism, people try to call them forth.

This distinction is quite clear and we must take it very seriously. If people were only to believe one thing I have said, I would like it to be this, that those who engage in spiritism — moving tables, séances, Ouija boards and other practices of that kind — think that they are summoning the souls of the dead. In reality, if there is some response to their call, it is always and without exception Satan and his angels who are answering.

People who practice spiritism (diviners, witches, etc.) are doing something very dangerous for themselves and for those who come to them for advice. They are up to their necks in lies. It is forbidden, strictly forbidden to call on the dead. As for me, I have never done so. I do not do so and I never will do so. When something appears to me, God alone permits it.

Of course, Satan can imitate everything that comes from God and he does. He can imitate a voice and the appearance of the dead, but every manifestation of any kind always comes from the evil one. Do not forget that Satan can even heal, but such healings never last.

Maria, have you personally ever been tricked by false apparitions? For example, by the devil disguising himself as a soul in Purgatory to speak to you?

Yes. Once a soul came to see me and said to me, "Do not accept the soul which is going to come after me, because it is going to ask you for too much suffering which you will not be able to bear. You cannot do what it is going to ask."

So, I was troubled, because I remembered what my parish priest had said to me, that I had to accept each soul with generosity and I was really troubled about whether or not to obey. So, I said to myself, "Maybe it is the devil who is appearing to me and not a soul in Purgatory, maybe the devil in disguise?" I said to this soul, "If you are the devil, go away!"

At once he gave a loud scream and left. In fact, the soul who came after him was a soul who had real need of my help. It was very important for me to listen to this soul!

When the devil appears, does Holy Water always make him leave?

It disturbs him very much and he flees at once.

Maria, you are now very well known, especially in Austria, Germany and throughout Europe. But at the beginning you were much hidden weren't you? How did it happen that overnight people recognized your supernatural experience as authentic?

It was when the souls asked me to tell their families to give back goods which had been acquired dishonestly. They saw that what I said was true.

At this point, Maria related several testimonies. Several times souls came to her, saying, "Go to my family in such and such a village, (which Maria, actually did not know about), and tell my father, tell my son, my brother, to give back a certain property or amount of money which I acquired dishonestly. I will be delivered from Purgatory when these goods are given back." Maria would know all the details of the field, the exact amount of money or the property concerned, and the family would be amazed to discover that she knew all these details, because sometimes even they did not know that these goods had been acquired dishonestly by their relative. Through this, Maria began to be very well known.

Maria, now I would like to ask you a question which might sound a little indiscrete. You have done so much for the poor souls that surely when you die in your turn, thousands of souls will be your escort into Heaven. I think that you certainly will not have to pass through Purgatory yourself?

I don't believe I will go straight to Heaven without time in Purgatory, because I have had more light, more knowledge and therefore my faults are more serious. But all the same, I hope that the souls will help me to rise to Heaven!

Certainly! And Maria, do you appreciate this charism, or is it something burdensome for you, all these requests from souls?

No, I don't pay much attention to the difficulty, for I know I can help them so much. I can help many souls and I am very happy to do this.

Maria, I would like to thank you from the heart for this
beautiful testimony, but please permit me one last question:
would you be so good as to tell us a few words about
your life?

Well... from when I was little, I wanted to enter a convent
but my mother told me to wait until I was twenty. I did
not wish to get married. My mother had told me a good
deal about the souls in Purgatory and already at school
these souls helped me a lot. So, I said to myself that I had
to do everything for them.

After school, I thought about entering a convent. I entered the Sisters of the Heart of Jesus, but they told me
that my health was too poor to stay with them. Actually,
as a child I had pneumonia and pleurisy. The superior had
confirmed my religious vocation but advised me to enter
an easier order and to wait for some years. I wanted above
all a cloistered order and right away.

But after two more attempts, the conclusion was
the same - my health was too poor. So, I said to myself
that entering a convent was not God's will for me. I
suffered mentally a great deal. I said to myself that the
Lord had not shown me what He wanted of me.

Up to the moment He entrusted me with this task for
the souls in Purgatory at the age of twenty-five, He had
made me wait eight years.

At home there were eight of us children. I worked on
our farm, starting at the age of fifteen. Then I went to

Germany as a servant for a peasant family. Afterwards, I worked here at the farm in Sonntag.

From the age of twenty-five, when the souls began to come, I had much to suffer for them. Now I am much better physically, so there you are . . .

This is the end of the interview with Maria.

A Few Notes
from Maria

"There is no value in complaining about the times that we live in. Parents do not help their children by responding to all their desires, by giving them everything that they want simply to keep them happy so that they don't have to listen to them yelling. Pride can take root in this way in the heart of the child. Later on, when the child starts school, he neither knows how to recite an Our Father nor how to make the sign of the Cross. In some cases, they know nothing about God.

Teach children how to make sacrifices! Why does religious indifference exist today? This moral decadence? Because children have not learned how to renounce their whims! They later on become misfits and people with no judgment, who get into all sorts of things and want to possess everything in abundance. This causes sexual deviations. This child who has not learned from its infancy to control himself, becomes selfish, hard hearted and even tyrannical. This is why today there is so much hatred and lack of charity. Do we want to live in a better time? Let us start by educating the children!

One sins very much against love of neighbor, especially by slander and gossip, deception and calumny. Where do these sins start? In the thoughts! We must learn these things from childhood and immediately drive out any uncharitable thoughts. Battle against all uncharitable thoughts, therefore, and one will then not judge others without charity.

This mission is homework for all Catholics. Some practice it through their profession, others through good example.

The preoccupation of the soul must not be extinguished by exaggerated care of the body . . ."

It was indeed a real pleasure for me to meet Maria Simma, a woman whose life is one of complete devotion. Each second, each hour of her life has a weight of eternity, not only for herself but for so many souls, known or unknown, that she in many different ways and with so much love has helped to deliver from Purgatory to enjoy the eternal happiness of Heaven.

The Saints speak to us about Purgatory

Several Saints have shed significant light on the reality of Purgatory. Thanks to their testimonies the faithful have concrete examples that illustrate and confirm the Doctrine of the Church.

We will peer into the writings of four saints in particular who are powerfully influencing our generation: St. Thérèse of the Child Jesus, St. Faustina Kowalska, St. Padre Pio, and St. Francis de Sales.

Saint Padre Pio

Do Not Delay!

Padre Pio told this story to Padre Anastasio, his fellow brother.

> "One evening, while I was alone in choir to pray, I heard the rustle of a suit and I saw a young monk that stirred next to the High Altar. It seemed that the young monk was dusting the candelabra and straightening the flower vases. I thought he was

Padre Leone rearranging the altar, and, since it was supper time, I went to him and I told him: 'Padre Leone, go to dinner, this is not the time to dust and to straighten the altar.'

But a voice, not Father Leone's, answered me: 'I am not Padre Leone.'

'And who are you?' I asked him.

'I am a brother of yours that made the novitiate here. I was ordered to clean the altar during the year of the novitiate. Unfortunately, many times I didn't reverence Jesus while passing in front of the altar, thus causing the Holy Sacrament that was preserved in the tabernacle to be disrespected. For this serious carelessness, I am still in Purgatory. Now, God, with His endless goodness, sent me here so that you may hasten the time I will enjoy Heaven. Pray for me!'

I believed I was being generous to that suffering soul, so I exclaimed: 'You will be in Paradise tomorrow morning, when I will celebrate Holy Mass.'

That soul cried: 'Cruel!'

Then he disappeared weeping.

That complaint produced in me a wound to the heart that I have felt and I will feel my whole life. In fact, I would have been able to immediately send that soul to Heaven but I condemned him to remain another night in the flames of Purgatory."

I Died in a Fire

One evening Padre Pio was on the ground floor of the convent, in a guestroom. He was alone. He had just lay down on the cot when, suddenly, a man appeared to him wrapped in a black cape. Padre Pio was amazed and arose to ask the man who he was and what he wanted. The stranger answered that he was a soul in Purgatory.

> "I am Pietro Di Mauro," he said. "I died in a fire on September 18, 1908, in this convent."

In fact, this convent, after the expropriation of the ecclesiastical goods, had been turned into a hospice for the elderly.

> "I died in the flames while I was sleeping on my straw mattress, right in this room. I have come from Purgatory. God has granted me to come here and ask you to say Mass for me tomorrow morning. Thanks to this Mass I will finally be able to enter into Paradise."

Padre Pio told the man that he would say Mass for him.

> "But," Padre Pio said, "I wanted to accompany him to the door of the convent. I realized I had spoken with a dead person. In fact, when we went out in the church square, the man that was at my side suddenly disappeared. I have to admit that I re- entered the convent rather frightened. Padre Paolino of Casacalenda, Superior of the convent, noticed my nervousness. After explaining to him what happened, I asked permission to celebrate Holy Mass for the deceased soul."

A few days later, Father Paolino, wanting to verify the information, went to the office of the registry of the commune of St. Giovanni Rotondo. He requested and was granted permission to consult the register of the deceased in the year 1908. The story of Father Pio was true. In the register of deaths, Father Paolino found that: "On September 18, 1908, in the fire of the hospice, Pietro Di Mauro died."

Cleonice's Mother

Mrs. Cleonice Morcaldi of St. Giovanni Rotondo was one of Padre Pio's spiritual daughters. One month after the death of her mother, Mrs. Cleonice went to confession with Padre Pio. After the confession he said to her: "This morning your mother has gone to Heaven. I have seen her while I was celebrating Holy Mass."

Like Little Flower and St. Faustina, Padre Pio could see beyond the tangible world. For him, there was no screen between Heaven, Purgatory and Earth. Precious are those witnesses who remind us of the spiritual world that our eyes cannot see but that is more real than our Television and computer screens.

St. Thérèse of the Child Jesus

St. Thérèse is the youngest Doctor of the Church. At a time when Catholic intellectuals were focusing on the justice of God, the Little Flower threw herself into the arms of God, whom she saw as her closest friend and most loving Father. Through her book, the Story of a Soul, she draws the Church into new depths of God's mercy.

In the Carmel of Lisieux, Sr. Maria Philomena was convinced that she would have to pass through Purgatory upon death. When she shared this with Little Thérèse, the Saint answered,

> "You do not have enough trust. You have too much fear before the good God. I can assure you that He is grieved over this. You should not fear purgatory because of the suffering there, but should instead ask that you do not deserve to go there in order to please God, who so reluctantly imposes this punishment. As soon as you try to please Him in everything and have an unshakeable trust, He purifies you every moment in His love and He lets no sin remain. And then you can be sure that you will not have to go to purgatory."

The Little Flower went even further than that — she truly thought that it was offending God if one didn't trust enough that he would go straight to heaven after death. When some of her Sisters expressed to her that they expected to go to purgatory, she exclaimed:

> "Oh, how you grieve me! You do a great injury to God in believing that you're going to Purgatory. When we love, we cannot go there!"

Thérèse of the Child Jesus was given the grace by God to see that Purgatory was not intended to be a rule but actually an exception. Doctrine teaches that everyone receives enough graces in order to go straight to God after passing the trials on earth. But Purgatory is an "emergency entry" to Heaven for those who have not grabbed God's grace for them.

Another time, one of her novices, Sr. Marie de la Trinité, said to her:

> "What if I fail even in the smallest thing, may I still hope to get straight to heaven?"

St. Thérèse, knowing the weaknesses of her novice, replied:

> "Yes! God is so good. He will know how to attract you to Him! But despite this, try to be faithful so that He does not wait in vain for your love."

Later, speaking about herself, Thérèse said:

> "I know that of myself I would not merit even to enter that place of expiation, since only holy souls can have entrance there. But I also know that the Fire of Love is more sanctifying than is the prison of Purgatory. I know that Jesus cannot desire useless sufferings for us, and that He would not inspire the longings I feel unless He wanted to grant them."

If the poor souls in Purgatory had known on earth what to expect in eternity, Purgatory would have remained empty!

Sr. Marie Febronia, sixty-seven, did not share the doctrine of Thérèse on Purgatory and found it presumptuous to believe that we could go straight to heaven. St. Thérèse, the youngest of the community, tried to explain her point of view to the elderly nun but to no avail. Finally, St. Thérèse said to her:

> "My Sister, if you want the justice of God, you will get it. A soul receives from God exactly what she expects from Him."

Less than a year later in January 1892, Sr. Febronia died. Three months later Sr. Thérèse had a dream. She told the dream to her Mother Prioress in these words: "Oh my mother, my Sister, Marie Febronia came to me last night and asked that we should pray for her. She's in Purgatory, surely because she had trusted too little in the mercy of the good God. Through her imploring behavior and profound looks, it seemed she wanted to say, 'You were right. I'm now delivered up to the full justice of God; but it is my fault. If I had listened to you, I would not be here now, I would have gone straight to Heaven.'

To her Sister Marie, Saint Thérèse wrote:

> "What pleases the Good God in me is that He sees me loving my littleness and my poverty, the blind hope that I have in His mercy. That is my only treasure, dear Godmother, why should this treasure not be yours?"

Saint Thérèse inspires us to have the boldness of a child when dealing with God. And doesn't the Kingdom of God belong to the children?

Saint Faustina Kowalska

Saint Faustina also exhorts us to blindly trust in the unfathomable mercy of God. It's not by chance that Pope John Paul II canonized Sister Faustina as the first saint in the Third Millennium! Her writings have spread like wild-fire meeting the needs of souls searching for Truth in today's society. In her Diary, Divine Mercy in My Soul, St. Faustina relates a few episodes that illustrate the link between Divine Mercy and Purgatory.

She writes:

> "When I entered the chapel for a moment, the Lord said to me, 'My daughter, help Me to save a dying sinner. Say the chaplet that I have taught you for him.' When I began to say the chaplet, I saw the man dying in the midst of terrible torment and struggle. His Guardian Angel was defending him, but he was, as it were, powerless against the enormity of the soul's misery. A multitude of devils was waiting for the soul. But while I was saying the chaplet, I saw Jesus just as He is depicted in the image (of the Merciful Christ). The rays which issued from Jesus' Heart enveloped the sick man, and the powers of darkness fled in panic. The sick man peacefully breathed his last. When I came back to my senses, I understood how very important the recitation of this chaplet was for the dying." (§ 1565).

In another circumstance, Saint Faustina shared what it is like for the souls in Purgatory to constantly thirst for God.

"I asked the Lord who else I should pray for. Jesus said: that on the following night he would let me know for whom I should pray. The next night I saw my Guardian Angel, who ordered me to follow him. In a moment I was in a misty place full of fire in which there was a great crowd of suffering souls. They were praying fervently, but to no avail for themselves. Only we can come to their aid. The flames which were burning them did not touch me at all. My Guardian Angel did not leave me for an instant. I asked these souls what their greatest suffering was. They answered me in one voice that their greatest torment was their longing for God. I saw Our Lady visiting the souls in purgatory. She brings them refreshment (…)" (§ 20)

Sister Faustina's charity exposed her to the torment some souls experience in Purgatory. She relates:

"July 9, 1937. This evening, one of the deceased Sisters came and asked me for one day of fasting and to offer all my (spiritual) exercises on that day for her. I answered that I would. From early morning on the following day, I offered everything for her intention. During Holy Mass, I had a brief experience of her torment. I experienced such intense hunger for God that I seemed to be dying of the desire to become united with Him. This lasted only a short time, but I understood what the longing of the souls in purgatory was like." (§ 1185 & 1186)

Nevertheless, it is possible that some souls, in their freedom, reject God until the end of their life and choose to live in eternity without Him. What happens to these souls? Saint Faustina provides us with one of the most striking descriptions of hell. She writes:

"Today I was led by an Angel to the chasms of Hell. It is a place of great torture; how awesomely large and extensive it is! The kinds of torture I saw: the first torture that constitutes hell is the loss of God; the second is perpetual remorse of conscience; the third is that one's condition will never change; the fourth is the fire that will penetrate the soul without destroying it — a terrible suffering, since it is a purely spiritual fire lit by God's anger; the fifth torture is continual darkness and a terrible suffocating smell, (despite the darkness the devils and the souls of the damned see each other and all the evil, both of others and their own); the sixth torture is the constant company of Satan; the seventh torture is horrible despair, hatred of God, vile words, curses and blasphemies. These are tortures suffered by all the damned together, but that is not the end of the sufferings. There are sufferings destined for particular souls. These are torments of the senses. Each soul undergoes terrible and indescribable sufferings related to the matter in which it has sinned. There are caverns and pits of torture where one form of agony differs from another. I would have died at the very sight of these tortures if the omnipotence of God had not supported me. Let the sinner know that he will be tortured throughout all eternity in those senses which he made use of to sin. I am writing this at the command of God so that no soul may find an excuse by saying there is no hell or that nobody has ever been there, and so no one can say what it is like.

I, Sister Faustina, by the order of God, have visited the abysses of hell so that I may tell souls about it and testify to its existence (...) The devils were full of hatred for me but they had to obey me at the command of God (...) I noticed one thing: that most of the souls there are those who disbelieved that there is a hell. When I came to my senses, I could hardly recover from the fright. How terribly souls suffer there. Consequently, I pray even more fervently for the conversion of sinners. I incessantly plead God's mercy upon them (...)" (§ 741)

"I often attend upon the dying and through entreaties obtain for them trust in God's mercy, and I implore God for an abundance of divine grace, which is always victorious. God's mercy sometimes touches the sinner at the last moment in a wondrous and mysterious way. Outwardly, it seems as if everything were lost, but it is not so. The soul, illuminated by a ray of God's powerful final grace, turns to God in the last moment with such a power of love that, in an instant, it receives from God forgiveness of sin and punishment, while outwardly it shows no sign either of repentance or of contrition, because souls (at that stage) no longer react to external things. Oh, how beyond comprehension is God's mercy! But — horror! — There are also souls who voluntarily and consciously reject and scorn this grace! Although a person is at the point of death, the merciful God gives the soul that interior vivid moment, so that if the soul is willing, it has the possibility of returning to God. But sometimes, the stubbornness in souls is so great that consciously they choose hell; they (thus) make useless all the prayers that other souls offer to God for them and even the efforts of God himself... (§1698)

(Extracts from the book "The Divine Mercy in my Soul," St. Faustina Diary, see *www.marian.org*)

Saint Francis de Sales

With reference to the words of Jesus in Mt 25: 35-40, Saint Francis de Sales wrote:

> "We forget too often our dear deceased ones. One willingly performs works of mercy, and one does not think of procuring the deliverance of the suffering souls when making this effort. Is it not a case of visiting those in prison? To deliver them? To lift the weight of their chains? Is it not a case of exercising hospitality, to help these children of God to enter the house of their Heavenly Father? You give clothes to the one who has none, you do good in this way; but it is even better to re-clothe in immortal splendor, these suffering members of the body of Christ."

A Proposition to All

Now my dear brothers and Sisters I have a proposition for all: we could make the decision that none of us will ever go to Purgatory, is this ok with you?

This is really possible. We have everything in our hands to make it come true. I remember the words of Saint John of the Cross who said that Divine Providence puts enough difficulties in our life — trials, sufferings, sicknesses, hardships — so that all these purifications may be enough to bring us straight to Heaven, of course if we accept them.

Why doesn't this happen? Because we rebel, we do not welcome with love, with gratitude, this gift of trials in our lives and we sin by rebelling, by not submitting, so to speak.

So, let's ask the Lord for the grace to seize every single opportunity so that on the day of our death, he sees us shining with purity and beauty.

Of course, if we decide on this, I do not say that the way will be easy, since the Lord never promised that the way would be easy, but that this way will be lived in peace and it will lead us to happiness. God will be with us. Above all — and this is what I would like to stress here — let's make the most of the time which remains to us on earth, this time which is so precious, during which we are still given the chance to grow in love. This means to grow towards the glory to come and the beauty which is destined for us. At each minute we can still grow in love, whereas for the souls in Purgatory, it is too late.

Even the angels in Heaven envy us for this power we have to grow each minute in love while we are still on earth.

Each little act of love we offer to God, each little sacrifice or fast, each little privation or battle against our tendencies or faults, each little forgiveness of our enemy, all the things we can offer of this sort will be an ornament for us later on, a jewel, a real treasure for eternity.

Then, let us seize every opportunity to be as beautiful as God desires us to be ultimately. Because if we saw in its full light, the splendor of an innocent soul, of a soul that is purified, then we would cry for joy and wonder at its beauty!

A human soul is something of great splendor before God; this is why God desires us to be perfectly pure; and it is not by being faultless in our ways that we will become pure. No, it is through repentance for our sins and through humility only. You see it is quite different! The saints are not faultless souls, but those who get up again and again, each time they fall and ask forgiveness. It is very different. Therefore, let's make use of the wonderful means the Lord puts into our hands. Let's help the souls still waiting to possess God and who yearn because of this delay. Imagine you are in their place. They have already seen this splendid God and they desire with all their heart to be with Him.

Also, we must not forget that the prayer of children has an immense power over the heart of God. So, let's teach our children to pray. I remember a little girl to whom I had spoken about the poor souls. I said to her, "Now you are going to pray for the souls of all the members of your family and friends who are already dead. Would you like to go before Jesus and ask Him?"

She went before Jesus and five minutes later she returned and I asked her, "What did you ask the Lord?"

She answered, "I asked the Lord to deliver all the souls in Purgatory!"

This answer struck me greatly and I realized that I had been miserly in my request but this little girl had understood straight away what to ask for. Children sense so much. They can obtain so much from the heart of God.

Also, let's mention the retired people and all those who have free time. If they went to Mass often, even daily, what a treasure of grace they would store up, not only for themselves but also for their deceased and for thousands of souls.

The value of one single Mass is immeasurable. If we only realized that…!

What riches our ignorance, our indifference, or simply our laziness leads us to waste!

Never forget, we have the power in our hands to help our brothers to be saved, together with Jesus our Saviour and Redeemer! Isn't this wonderful!

Prayers for the deceased

O Divine Heart of Jesus

Grant me the grace always to live according to your will as much in the finest, most important moments of my life as in the difficult moments.

Grant me always to be ready for my last hour, give me the courage to give everything for your love, even my life if necessary.

Jesus through your most Holy and painful Passion, may your coming at the hour of my death, find me awake, like a good servant with true repentance, a good confession, fortified by the last sacraments.

Lord do not abandon me in my last struggle on this earth, when I will have to battle against Satan, perhaps raging in fury. May your Holy Mother, the Mother of Mercy, and Saint Michael and all the angels help and protect me against all temptation in the hour when I leave this world. May they strengthen and console me in my pain.

Grant me Lord at that hour a living faith, a firm trust, an ardent love and a great patience.

Help me to commit myself fully in all clarity of mind into your hands and to abandon myself like a little child to your holy peace.

In your infinite goodness and your great mercy, oh Jesus, remember me! Amen.

Psalm 129

Out of the depths I cry to You, O Lord; Lord, hear my voice.

Let Your ears be attentive to my voice in supplication. If You, O Lord, mark iniquities, Lord, who can stand? But with You is forgiveness, that You may be revered. I trust in the Lord; my soul trusts in His word.

My soul waits for the Lord more than sentinels wait for the dawn.

More than sentinels wait for the dawn, let Israel wait for the Lord,

For with the Lord is kindness and with Him is plenteous redemption;

And He will redeem Israel from all their iniquities.

Prayer of Saint Mechtilde for the Deceased

Our Father who art in Heaven; I beseech You, O Heavenly Father, pardon the Souls in Purgatory, for they did not love You sufficiently, nor render to You all the honor which is Your due, due to You their Lord and Father, Who, by pure grace, have adopted them as Your children. By their sins, rather, have they driven You from their souls, where You none the less wished always to live. In reparation for these faults, I offer You the love and veneration which Your Incarnate Son showed You all during His earthly life, and I offer all the acts of penance and satisfaction which He performed and by which He effaced and atoned for the sins of men.

Hallowed be thy name; I beg You, O Father Most Good, pardon the Souls in Purgatory, for they did not honor, always and fittingly, Your Holy Name, but often they took It in vain and proved unworthy of the name "Christian," by their lives of sin. In reparation for their faults, I offer to You all the honor which Your Well-Beloved Son rendered to Your Name by His words and deeds.

Thy Kingdom come; I pray You, Father Most Good, pardon the Souls in Purgatory, for they did not always seek or adore Your Kingdom with enough fervor and diligence; This Kingdom, the only place where true rest and peace reign. In reparation for their omissions, through indifference to do what is good, I offer You the Most Holy Desire of Your Son, by which He wished that they also might become heirs of His Kingdom.

Thy will be done on earth as it is in Heaven; I pray You, Father Most Good, pardon the Souls in Purgatory, for they did not always submit their will to Your Will. In reparation for their disobedience, I offer You the perfect conformity of the Heart, full of love, of Your Divine Son with Your Holy Will and the most profound submission which He showed in obeying You unto death on the Cross.

Give us this day our daily bread; I pray You, Father Most Good, pardon the Souls in Purgatory, for they did not always receive the Holy Sacrament of the Eucharist with enough desire, but often without contemplation, or love, or even unworthily, or they neglected to receive It. In reparation for these faults, I offer You the outstanding Holiness and the great contemplation of Our Lord Jesus Christ, Your Divine Son, addressed to You in favor of His enemies when He was on the Cross.

Forgive us our trespasses as we forgive those who trespass against us; I pray You, Father Most Good, pardon the Souls in Purgatory, all the faults of which they have been guilty through succumbing to the Seven Capital Sins and also in not having wished either to love or pardon their enemies. In reparation for these faults, I offer You the outstanding Holiness and the great contemplation of Our Lord Jesus Christ, Your Divine Son, addressed to You in favor of His enemies when He was on the Cross.

And lead us not into temptation; I pray You, Father Most Good, pardon the Souls in Purgatory, because too often they did not resist temptations and the passions, but they followed the Enemy of all goodness. In reparation for all these sins, in thought, word, and deed. I offer You the glorious victory which Our Lord won against the world, as well as His Most Holy Life, His Work and Sorrows, His Suffering and His Most Cruel Death.

But deliver us from evil; and from all punishments through the Infinite Merits of Your Well-Beloved Son and lead us, as well as the Souls in Purgatory, into Your Kingdom of eternal glory. Amen.

Rosary for the 100 Requiem for the Souls in Purgatory

Ana Maria Taigi was very devoted to the souls in Purgatory. She was generous in giving suffrages to the souls by praying 100 Requiem. She testifies that through this prayer she obtains many heavenly favors in different circumstances and for various needs.

In the name of the Father, and of the Son, and of the Holy Spirit. Amen.

My Jesus, I offer you for the benefit of the souls in Purgatory, the merits of your sufferings endured for our redemption. I start by contemplating the Blood that oozed out from your

Body due to the sadness and anguish that you experienced in the Garden of Gethsemane.

Eternal rest, grant unto them, O Lord, and let perpetual light shine upon them.

May they rest in peace. Amen. (10 times)

Holy souls of Purgatory, pray to God for me and I will ask the Father to give you the glory of Paradise.

My Jesus, I offer you for the souls of Purgatory, the admirable patience with which You endure the tortures of those vile soldiers who led you to Annas, Caiaphas, Pilate, and Herod, to give you more insult they dressed you up in purple amid the mockeries and insults of the people.

Eternal rest, grant unto them, O Lord... (10 times)

Holy souls of Purgatory, pray to God for me and I will ask the Father to give you the glory of Paradise.

My Jesus, I offer you for the souls of Purgatory, the bitterness you felt when they chose Barabbas, who was a criminal, instead of you, the innocent one. Later on, tied to a pillar, You were scourged without mercy.

Eternal rest, grant unto them, O Lord... (10 times)

Holy souls of Purgatory, pray to God for me and I will ask the Father to give you the glory of Paradise.

My Jesus, I offer you for the souls of Purgatory, the humiliation you suffered when, treating you as a false king, they put on your shoulders a purple cloak gave you a stick for your sceptre, and crowned your head with thorns, and in this way Pilate presented you to the mob saying: Look at this man!

Eternal rest, grant unto them, O Lord... (10 times)

Holy souls of Purgatory, pray to God for me and I will ask the Father to give you the glory of Paradise.

My Jesus, I offer you for the souls of Purgatory, the intense sorrow you felt when the mob shouted: "Crucify him!" and when the heavy burden of the cross made you stumble several times as you carried it to Mt. Calvary.

Eternal rest, grant unto them, O Lord... (10 times)

Holy souls of Purgatory, pray to God for me and I will ask the Father to give you the glory of Paradise.

My Jesus, I offer you for the souls of Purgatory, the compassion and deep pain You felt when you were separated violently from Your beloved Mother who came to meet and embrace you on your way to Calvary.

Eternal rest, grant unto them, O Lord... (10 times)

Holy souls of Purgatory, pray to God for me and I will ask the Father to give you the glory of Paradise.

My Jesus, I offer you for the souls of Purgatory the untold torments you endured when your bloody body was extended on the cross and they nailed your hands and feet to it, and they raised up the cross violently and planted it in a hole.

Eternal rest, grant unto them, O Lord... (10 times)

Holy souls of Purgatory, pray to God for me and I will ask the Father to give you the glory of Paradise.

My Jesus, I offer you for the souls of Purgatory the anguish and pains that, for three hours, you endured while hanging on the cross, made more painful by your knowing that your sorrowful Mother was there beneath your cross.

Eternal rest, grant unto them, O Lord... (10 times)

Holy souls of Purgatory, pray to God for me and I will ask the Father to give you the glory of Paradise.

My Jesus, I offer you for the souls of Purgatory the desolation that your Mother endured when she saw you dead, and when your body was lowered down from the cross and she embraced and carried Your lifeless body.

Eternal rest, grant unto them, O Lord... (10 times)

Holy souls of Purgatory, pray to God for me and I will ask the Father to give you the glory of Paradise.

The Holy Wounds for the Souls in Purgatory

Here are the promises made by Jesus to Sister Marie Marthe Chambon (1841-1907), a humble converse Sister of the Monastery of the Visitation of Santander, who died in the odor of sanctity. A daughter of poor peasants, she entered the monastery in 1864. After a vision of Jesus on the cross who shed his blood, she consecrated herself to the Holy Wounds of Jesus, of which she had impressive visions every day. In 1875, she received the stigmata.

a) "I shall grant all that will be requested of me through the invocation of my Holy Wounds. You need to spread this devotion."

b) "In truth, this prayer does not come from earth, but from Heaven.... and it can obtain everything.

c) "My Holy Wounds sustain the world... ask Me that you may love them always, because they are the source of grace. One must invoke them often, and draw one's neighbor to them in order to impress in their heart the devotion for souls.

d) "When you experience some sorrow, or have something to suffer, you need to bring it hastily into my Wounds, and your sorrow shall be softened."

"You have to often repeat before the sick this invocation: "My Jesus, pardon and mercy, through the merits of thy Holy Wounds! "This prayer shall soothe both the soul and body."

e) "The sinner who will say the following prayer: "Eternal Father, I offer thee the Wounds of Our Lord Jesus Christ to heal those of our souls," shall obtain his own conversion."

"My Wounds shall repair yours."

f) "There shall be no death for the soul who will expire in my Wounds: they give true life."

g) "With every word of the Chaplet of Mercy you pronounce, I let a drop of my blood fall on the soul of a sinner."

h) "The soul which honors my Holy Wounds and offers them to the Eternal Father for the souls in Purgatory, will be accompanied towards death by the very Holy Virgin and by the Angels and I Myself, resplendent in glory, I will receive them to crown them.

i) "The Holy Wounds are a treasure for the souls in Purgatory.

j) "The devotion to my Holy Wounds is the remedy for this time of sinfulness.

"From my Wounds come the fruit of holiness.

k) "You shall obtain all things, because it is the merit of my Blood which is of an infinite price."

l) "With my Wounds and my Divine Heart, you can obtain all things."

m) "Offer me your actions... united to my Holy Wounds, there are incomprehensible riches, even into the least ones."

n) "It is necessary to expire while kissing these sacred Wounds."

o) "The way of my Wounds is so simple, so easy to reach Heaven!…"

p) "My Wounds shall cover all your faults." "Offer them to me often for sinners, for: I thirst for souls."

q) "This Chaplet of Mercy balances my Justice; it stops my vengeance."

Rosary of the Holy Wounds of Our Lord Jesus Christ

You can recite this rosary (of mercy) on a normal rosary and begin the prayer as follows;

a. O Jesus, Divine Redeemer, be merciful to us and to the whole world. Amen.

b. God powerful, God holy, God immortal, have mercy on us and on the whole world. Amen.

c. Grace, mercy, my Jesus during the present dangers; cover us with thy Precious Blood. Amen.

d. Eternal Father, grant us mercy through the Blood of Jesus Christ, thy only Son; grant us mercy, we beseech thee. Amen.

On the *Our Father* beads, say;

Eternal Father, I offer thee the Wounds of Our Lord Jesus Christ, to heal those of our souls.

On the *Hail Mary* beads, say;

My Jesus, pardon and mercy, through the merits of thy Holy Wounds.

At the end of the rosary, repeat three times:

Eternal Father, I offer thee the Wounds of Our Lord Jesus Christ, to heals those of our souls.

Divine Mercy Chaplet

In 1937 Jesus dictated to St. Faustina Kowalska a novena to the Divine Mercy. Each day Sr. Faustina brought to Jesus' heart a different group of souls and immersed them in the ocean of His Mercy. The eighth day of the novena is dedicated to the souls in Purgatory. Jesus presented it this way:

> 1226: "Today bring to Me the souls who are in the prison of Purgatory, and immerse them in the abyss of My mercy. Let the torrents of My Blood cool down their scorching flames. All these souls are greatly loved by Me. They are making retribution to My justice. It is in your power to bring them relief. Draw all the indulgences from the treasury of My Church and offer them on their behalf. Oh, if you only knew the torments they suffer, you would continually offer for them the alms of the spirit and pay off their debt to My justice."

Most Merciful Jesus, You Yourself have said that You desire mercy; so I bring into the abode of Your Most Compassionate Heart the souls in Purgatory, souls who are very dear to You and yet who must make, retribution to Your justice. May the streams of Blood and Water which gushed forth from Your Heart put out the flames of the purifying fire, that in that place, too, the power of Your mercy may be praised.

From the terrible heat of the cleansing fire rises a plaint to Your mercy,

And they receive comfort, refreshment, relief in the stream of mingled Blood and Water.

Eternal Father, turn Your merciful gaze upon the souls suffering in Purgatory, who are enfolded in the Most Compassionate Heart of Jesus. I beg You, by the sorrowful Passion of Jesus Your Son, and by all the bitterness with which His most sacred Soul was flooded, manifest Your mercy to the souls who are under Your just scrutiny. Look upon them in no other way than through the Wounds of Jesus, Your dearly beloved Son; for we firmly believe that there is no limit to Your goodness and compassion."

The Chaplet of Divine Mercy

(Recited using the beads of the rosary)

To begin;

One Our Father..., Hail Mary..., Apostles Creed.

Recite on the 'Our Father' beads;

Eternal Father, I offer you the body and blood, soul and divinity of Your dearly beloved Son, our Lord Jesus Christ, in atonement for our sins and those of the whole world.

Recite on the 'Hail Mary' beads;

For the sake of His sorrowful Passion, have mercy on us and on the whole world.

Recite at the end, three times;

Holy God, Holy Mighty One, Holy Immortal One, have mercy on us and on the whole world.

Don't Forget about Indulgences

Mother Church has some wonderful treasures in store for us — let's take a closer look at some of them!

> "Through indulgences the faithful can obtain the remission of temporal punishment resulting from sins for themselves and also for the souls in Purgatory." (Catechism of the Catholic Church, § 1498)

What is an indulgence? Here is what the Catechism of the Catholic Church has to say:

> "An indulgence is a remission before God of the temporal punishment due to sins whose guilt has already been forgiven, which the faithful Christian who is duly disposed gains under certain prescribed conditions through the action of the Church which, as the minister of redemption, dispenses and applies with authority the treasury of the satisfactions of Christ and the saints.

> "An indulgence is partial or plenary according as it removes either part or all of the temporal punishment due to sin. Indulgences may be applied to the living or the dead." (§ 1471)

Jesus gave to his disciples, and therefore to the Church, the power to bind and to loose, and down through the centuries, in many different ways, the Church has used this channel of the mercy of God towards the living and the dead.

Everything concerning indulgences was revised by Pope Paul VI; the results can be found in The Book of Indulgences, Rules and Grants, published June 29, 1968 (Vatican Publishers).

> "The aim pursued by ecclesiastical authority in granting indulgences is not only that of helping the faithful to expiate the punishment due to sin, but also that of urging them to perform works of piety, penitence and charity — particularly those which lead to growth in faith and which favour the common good."

> "And if the faithful offer indulgences in suffrage for the dead, they cultivate charity in an excellent way and while raising their minds to heaven they bring a wiser order into the things of this world."

> "Although indulgences are in fact free gifts, nevertheless they are granted for the living as well as for the dead only on determined conditions... the faithful have to love God, detest sin, place their trust in the merits of Christ and believe firmly in the great assistance they derive from the communion of saints."

As a result of the reform, all distinctions of day, month, and year have been abolished; the only distinction retained is that between plenary and partial indulgence.

We should also note the following:

> • No one can give the indulgence he obtains to another person who is still living.

> • Both plenary and partial indulgences can always be given for the dead.

> The faithful who use with devotion an object of piety (crucifix, cross, rosary, scapular or medal) properly blessed by any priest, can acquire a partial indulgence. But if this object is blessed by the Supreme Pontiff or any bishop, the faithful who use it devoutly can also acquire a plenary indulgence on the feast of the Holy Apostles Peter and Paul, provided they also make a profession of faith using any legitimate formula."

In Medjugorje, on July 18 1995, Our Lady said:

> "Dear children, today I call you to place more blessed objects in your homes and call everyone to put some blessed object on their person. Bless all objects, and thus Satan will attack you less because you will have armour against him."

> "To acquire a plenary indulgence, it is necessary to perform the work to which the indulgence is attached and to fulfill three conditions: sacramental confession, Eucharistic Communion and prayer for the intentions of the Supreme Pontiff. It is further required that all attachment to sin, even venial sin, be absent."

The condition of praying for the Supreme Pontiff's intention is fully satisfied by reciting one "Our Father" and one "Hail Mary." Nevertheless, the individual faithful are free to recite any other prayer according to their own piety and devotion toward the Supreme Pontiff.

The new reform provides for three concessions:

1. Partial indulgence is granted to the faithful who, in fulfilling their duties and in facing the adversities of life, raise their soul to God with humble confidence, and add in their heart a pious invocation.

2. Partial indulgence is granted to the faithful who, with a soul full of faith and mercy, give themselves or their goods to their brothers in need.

3. Partial indulgence is granted to the faithful who, in a spirit of repentance, deprive themselves spontaneously of something.

Plenary indulgence can be obtained on the following occasions:

• Adoration of the Blessed Sacrament for at least one half-hour;

• Recitation of the entire rosary in church, as a family or in community;

• Making the Stations of the Cross;

• Reading Holy Scripture for at least one half-hour;

• A Church visit between noon of November 1 and midnight of November 2, for the intention of the deceased;

• Visiting a cemetery, for the intention of the deceased;

• Taking part in a First Holy communion ceremony, or the first Mass of a priest, or the anniversary of 25, 50, or 60 years of priesthood;

• Renewing one's baptismal promises during the Easter Vigil;

• Adoration of the Cross during the Good Friday liturgy;

• Papal benediction, even when received listening to the radio or watching on television.

By going to confession regularly, one can obtain many plenary indulgences.

Only one plenary indulgence a day is permitted, but one may obtain a number of partial indulgences on one day by reciting certain prayers suggested by the Church, such as:

• To you, Blessed Joseph

• Angelus Domini

• Soul of Christ, sanctify me

• Act of Spiritual Communion

• The Creed

• The Office of the Dead

• Psalm 130 (De profundis)

• Litanies of the Most Holy Name of Jesus

• Litanies of the Sacred Heart of Jesus

- Litanies of the Most Precious Blood

- Litanies of the Blessed Virgin Mary

- Litanies of Saint Joseph

- Litanies of the Saints

- Magnificat

- Remember, O most gracious Virgin Mary

- Psalm 51 (Miserere)

- Prayer for priestly or religious vocations

- Prayer for Unity of the Christians

- Salve Regina (Hail, Holy Queen)

- Sign of the Cross (devoutly done)

- Tantum ergo (Let us adore the Sacrament)

- Te Deum

- Veni Creator (Come, Holy Spirit)

There are other prayers not listed here.

Partial indulgences are obtained through concrete acts of faith, hope, and love, in the midst of the trials of life and as we carry out the duties of our daily lives. Indulgences are also obtained by acts of charity towards our neighbour, voluntary fasting, and ejaculatory prayers or spontaneous thoughts addressed to God, to the Blessed Mother, to the Holy Family.

The Book of Indulgences contains a list of suggested prayers; it is a precious book — read it!

Other Titles by the Same Author

The Forgotten Power of Fasting
HEALING, LIBERATION, JOY …

"I read your book from cover to cover. Your words completely captivated me and have convinced me on the importance of fasting. I knew already the benefits of fasting, but I wasn't aware of all its attributes, that you explain so well. Reading this book one discovers fasting.

As we know, Our Lady in Medjugorje continuously insists on the importance of fasting, but we avoid putting into practice something when it means we have to make a sacrifice. We struggle to convince ourselves to actually fast.

The arguments you present, and the examples that you give in this book, show very clearly the reason why Our Lady insists so persistently on something so precious for the soul and the body, for the apostolate on earth and for the souls in Purgatory. I thank you for emphasizing such an important topic, very often mentioned in Sacred Scripture, so precious for the living and for the intercession of the dead.

The final part of your work, with the words from the saints, will convince even the most reluctant.

This book will be nothing less than a true discovery of fasting to whoever reads it."

Don Gabriele Amorth

Euro 7.00
Sister Emmanuel
© 1995 Children of Medjugorje
www.sremmanuel.org

Children, Help My Heart To Triumph!

At the height of the Bosnian War, Sister Emmanuel remained in Medjugorje with a few members of her community. During that time, memories of her father, a Prisoner of War during WWII, continually surfaced. Remembering how much he suffered, she felt a need to do something to spiritually help those on the front lines. Sister Emmanuel describes a call that she received at that time to appeal to the children for their sacrifices in order to alleviate the war. *Children, Help My Heart To Triumph* was written in response to that call. It describes for children how to make a 9-day novena of little sacrifices. Included is a coloring book that they can color and mail to Medjugorje where they will be presented at one of Our Lady's apparitions.

US $ 11.99
Sister Emmanuel
© 1996 Children of Medjugorje
Reprinted 2012 Includes Coloring Book
www.sremmanuel.org

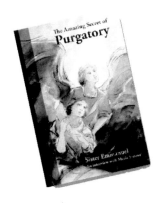

The Amazing Secret of the Souls in Purgatory

It is not often that a book touches the soul so deeply. *The Amazing Secret of the Souls in Purgatory* is such a book. Maria Simma, deceased in March of 2003, lived a humble life in the mountains of Austria. When she was twenty-five, Maria was graced with a very special charism—the charism of being visited by the many souls in Purgatory—and being able to communicate with them! Maria shares, in her own words, some amazing secrets about the souls in Purgatory. She answers questions such as: What is Purgatory? How do souls get there? Who decides if a soul goes to Purgatory? How can we help get souls released from Purgatory?

US $ 8.99

© 1997 Queenship Publishing

www.queenship.org

www.sremmanuel.org

The Hidden Child of Medjugorje

"Reading "Medjugorje, the 90s" had left me dazzled and so deeply touched that it had literally pulled me to Medjugorje. I just had to see with my own eyes the spiritual wonders retold in that book. Now with "The Hidden Child," the ember of love for Mary has received a new breath of air—a Pentecostal wind. Sr. Emmanuel is indeed one of Mary's best voices! Congratulations for this jewel of a testimonial! I wouldn't be surprised if the Gospa herself turned out to be Sister's most avid reader."

Msgr. Denis Croteau, OMI

"Books are like seashells; at first they all look alike. However, they are far from being identical and their value varies greatly. Some of them are packed with riches and so well written, that they hide rare pearls within. Sister Emmanuel's book is one of those; it contains the most beautiful pearls, and with them enriches the reader. Through her accounts and anecdotes, the reader is pleased to meet people of great worth and to be filled with the teachings of so many events. Through this book, one will explore more fully a way still too little known: the way of the Queen of Peace."

Fr. Jozo Zovko, OFM

US $ 15.99
Sister Emmanuel
© 2010 Children of Medjugorje, Inc.
www.sremmanuel.org

Maryam of Bethlehem, the Little Arab

Who is this little Arab? Maryam Baouardy is a daughter of Galilee. Her life? A succession of supernatural manifestations worthy of Catherine of Sienna. Maryam shares the keys of holiness, including ways to defeat Satan himself. This is a book you don't want to miss?

US $ 5.00

Sister Emmanuel

© 2012 Children of Medjugorje, Inc.

www.sremmanuel.org

Available in E-Book

The Beautiful Story of Medjugorje
As Told to Children from 7 to 97

In this book, you will follow the experiences of six little shepherds, their shock when they saw the "Lady" appearing to them in 1981. You will see how Vicka and Jokov actually experienced the reality of life beyond this world, when Our Lady took them with her on the most extraordinary journey to Heaven, Purgatory and Hell.

You will learn how brave they were under persecution. You will be excited to know the mes—sages they share from a Mother who thinks only of helping us, who loves each one of us so much—including you in a very special way!

You will read about the powerful healings of bodies and souls happening there, as in Lourdes.

This is an adventure story, except that this story is true and is happening right now for you!

US $ 5.00
Sister Emmanuel
© 2012 Children of Medjugorje
www.sremmanuel.org
Available in E-Book

Peace will have the last word

The mercy of God is scandalous, it even borders on the extreme! In her engaging and lively style, Sister Emmanuel recounts real life stories and testimonies that take the reader's heart on a journey of God's mercy, passing through the prisons of New York, and into the confessionals of the Saints!

In these pages, a mosaic of photos and parables, the reader encounters the very depths of the human heart and is transported into the midst of scenes and situations that are as captivating as they are diverse. Through them we witness that much-desired peace that comes from Above, gaining victory over emptiness, futility and fear.

Here are words that many no longer dare to speak, and yet, they have the power to help rebuild a degenerating society. This book is a shot in the arm, an injection of hope that will hasten the time when, in the hearts of all, peace will have the last word!

US $ 13.99
Sister Emmanuel
© 2015 Children of Medjugorje
www.sremmanuel.org

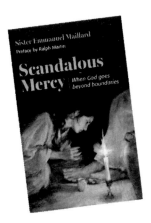

Scandalous Mercy
WHEN GOD GOES BEYOND THE BOUNDARIES

Why Scandalous Mercy?

In these pages the reader will discover unexplored aspects of the Heart of God that you might think are crazy! Crazy with love! You will meet Mother Teresa, Maryam of Bethlehem, a Nazi criminal, a priest condemned to hell, a high ranking abortionist, a drug dealer from Brazil, a furious mother-in-law, a sick child…and in the middle of all this, the most beautiful Heart of Christ, who is calling ALL His children.

This beautiful selection of testimonies and "little flowers" picked from everyday life will capture the reader on two levels: first, the reader of this book will find his achy heart soothed and enriched by new ways to find hope in our difficult world today; second, he will be shocked to learn that these stories are true. They will make you laugh, cry, even tremble, but one thing is certain, they will all amaze you!

US $ 13.00
Sister Emmanuel
© 2015 Children of Medjugorje
www.sremmanuel.org

Medjugorje, Triumph of the Heart
REVISED EDITION OF MEDJUGORJE OF THE 90S

Sister Emmanuel offers a pure echo of Medjugorje, the eventful village where the Mother of God has been appearing since 1981. She shares at length some of the personal stories of the villagers, the visionaries, and the pilgrims who flock there by the thousands, receiving great healings. Eight years of awe have inspired this book. these 89 stories offer a glimpse into the miracles of Mary's motherly love.

US $ 12.95
Sister Emmanuel
© 2015 Children of Medjugorje
www.sremmanuel.org

Manufactured by Amazon.ca
Acheson, AB